# WINE JOURNAL

## A WINE LOVER'S ALBUM FOR CELLARING AND TASTING

TEXT BY GERALD ASHER

PHOTOGRAPHS BY STEVEN ROTHFELD

**CollinsPublishers**

*A Division of* HarperCollins*Publishers*

GERALD ASHER is the Wine Editor of *Gourmet* magazine, where he contributes a monthly column, as well as occasional travel articles. He has been published extensively in books, periodicals and newspapers on both sides of the Atlantic. Trained in the wine trade in England, Spain, Germany and France, he has managed wine ventures in London, New York and San Francisco. He has been inducted into numerous wine fraternities, and honored for both his writing and for his work in the international wine trade. In 1974, he was decorated by the French government with the star and ribbon of the Mérite Agricole for services to French agriculture. Since 1972, he has contributed essays to *Gourmet,* a collection of which, entitled *On Wine,* was published in 1982. A further collection will be published in the fall of 1996. He divides his time between San Francisco and Paris.

STEVEN ROTHFELD has created the images for several books including *Italian Dreams* (Collins, 1996), *Savoring the Wine Country* (Collins, 1995), *French Dreams* (Workman, 1994) and Patricia Wells' *Trattoria* (Morrow, 1993). His work has appeared in *European Travel & Life, Bon Appetit, Departures* and *Travel & Leisure* magazines and is represented by the Gallery of Contemporary Photography in Santa Monica, California.

First published in the USA 1996 by Collins Publishers San Francisco
Copyright © 1996 Collins Publishers San Francisco
Text copyright © 1996 Gerald Asher
The introduction on p. 6 was originally published in *Gourmet* magazine,
copyright © 1995 Gerald Asher. Reprinted with permission.
The following photographs are reprinted with permission from *Savoring the Wine Country,* copyright © 1995 by Steven Rothfeld: cover, pp. 1, 6, 11, 14, 17, 24, 80, 88, 97, 104, 112
Photographs copyright © 1996 by Steven Rothfeld: pp. 2, 32, 40, 48, 56, 64, 72, 94, 128
Design: Kari Perin
Editor: Meesha Halm,
Design/Production Coordination: Kristen Wurz
HarperCollins Web Site: hhtp://www.harpercollins.com
HarperCollins Publishers Inc., 📖® and CollinsPublishers™ are trademarks of HarperCollins Publishers Inc.
Printed in Hong Kong  10 9 8 7 6 5

# CONTENTS

# INTRODUCTION

Starting a wine cellar is not the same thing as buying wine to keep in the house. Some might wonder about the distinction and even question the word *cellar*—with its image of candles and cobwebbed vaults—as being more than a shade pretentious when applied to the nooks and crannies where an average apartment dweller might hoard supplies of wine. So let me say right away that the word *cellar* comes to us from a Latin expression used to designate a small space reserved for storage. When we use it to describe the contents of a few cartons set on their sides in a coat closet, we're closer to its original meaning than when we refer to underground galleries where thousands upon thousands of bottles gather dust.

The impulse to get started often comes from the acquisition of a case or two of some fine but young Bordeaux or of a much-praised Cabernet Sauvignon that we are assured will need several years of nurturing. We put it away but the time inevitably arrives when this friend or that is expected to dinner and there's no other wine in the house. "Well, we can open a bottle of Château Sleeper and see how it's coming along" seems a reasonable enough solution. It happens again, and sooner than one would imagine the tannin-laden chrysalides that were supposed to emerge as butterflies have all disappeared before their wings were even formed. That's why it's best to begin by deciding what one's immediate needs are and then organize a revolving stock of wine to meet them.

Even in a cellar composed essentially for current use, there's usually room enough to set aside a few bottles to age for some special occasion —a significant anniversary or an ominously round-numbered birthday. Those who want well-aged wines in their cellars on a regular basis will, however, have to be patient (unless they can invest immediately in mature wines, most reliably found at the auction houses) and build on a long-term stock to which they add when opportune.

Lack of space is no bar to holding wine for future consumption when commercial storage facilities are available. In many cities they are often associated with a local wine merchant, a retailer who will usually be able to help customers make suitable arrangements. If wine is to be kept where it's likely to become confused with the property of the merchant or others, it is prudent to mark every box and carton directly and indelibly with your name (don't rely on attached labels) to avoid possible dispute in the event of a business failure. The warehouse—even if it belongs to a wine merchant—should be visited before any stock is consigned there. It's not wise to assume that all who are professionally involved with wine store it under perfect or even satisfactory conditions.

What conditions *are* satisfactory? Ideally, wine should be kept— bottles on their sides, of course, to keep the corks moist—in a dark place where there is little danger of its being disturbed and at a temperature close to 55°F. That's the temperature intended when we are urged to drink a wine "cellar cool." Wines mature more quickly between 65°F and 70°F and therefore, it is thought, risk missing the peak attained by wines allowed to evolve more slowly. In the short term, however, harm is less likely at this slightly warmer temperature —and easier for most of us to manage anyway—provided it's constant, than at a lower one that is less stable. A widely fluctuating temperature is a menace. When the temperature rises, wine expands in the bottle and will sometimes even push the cork up slightly. Whether the cork moves or not, the wine's volume contracts as the temperature falls again, and the vacuum left behind the cork sucks air into the bottle, exposing the wine to oxidation and premature aging.

For people whose houses or apartments are not too severely affected by seasonal extremes and the abrupt changes imposed by central heating and air-conditioning, a basement, insulated from both the outside and from any furnace or hot-water pipes, will probably be suitable for wine storage. (A minimum/maximum thermometer will soon reveal unsuspected problems.) Failing that, a dark closet—light is harmful to wine—insulated as best one can will probably serve adequately. With little trouble and at modest expense, basement or closet can be fitted with modular bottle racks. Racks of wood slats or wire, made to measure, are available through a number of mail-order companies and allow considerable quantities of wine to be stowed in quite small spaces. Several companies publish illustrated catalogues with a good variety. Two reputable sources are The Wine Enthusiast (P.O. Box 39, Pleasantville, NY 10570) and International Wine Accessories (11020 Audelia Road, Suite B 113, Dallas, TX 75243; 1-800-527-4072).

These companies also sell temperature-controlled wine cabinets, including some disguised as dining-room furniture and others that will hold more than fifty dozen bottles in an upright two-door armoire of generous proportions. Though expensive, these chests offer a sensible, if not particularly graceful, solution when there seems to be no other.

The choice of wine should be one's own, of course, reflecting personal tastes and preferences. Books and articles that propose "ideal cellars" in which there are representative bottles from every major wine region can be—should be—ignored. We are better off thinking less about all the world's wines and more about what we expect to do with those we have. As it evolves, a cellar is shaped in any case by the nature of the occasions (or non-occasions) on which the wine is drunk, the food most often eaten with it, the amount of money we have to spend, the storage space available, and the rate at which bottles are opened. Choices change with the seasons, almost certainly, as well as with our enthusiasms and chance discoveries of new wines. As wines vary from vintage to vintage, something we revel in one year might be less appealing the next. So the collection is sure to be somewhat organic, modifying itself every time we replenish it.

Except on the most formal occasions, most of us use wine fairly casually. A bottle is opened as friends arrive for dinner, or before we all go out to a movie. The wines we drink regularly, the basic favorites of the cellar, red or white, that we drink on most days—with solo meals, family meals, and informal meals with friends—must adapt easily to the foods we like to eat without any fussing about perfect matches. Otherwise, how can anyone finish with a salad lunch the wine that was started with last night's *osso buco*? Wines for special celebrations, whether drawn from our reserves of mature vintages (if there are any), or purchased as needed, are expected to fit the occasion and the food and to warm the hearts of friends invited to share them with us.

We each have a favorite white wine for incidental and aperitif use. It should have enough fragrance and flavor to be interesting independently of food. In fact, the best wines for the purpose are often those difficult to fit with food—Gewürztraminers, Viogniers, exceedingly aromatic Sauvignon Blancs. Light and flowery Moselles, otherwise hard to accommodate but always a pleasure to drink, also fit this role well.

Whatever the choice of white wine, I recommend your making room in the refrigerator for a bottle of the least expensive sparkling wine you really *enjoy*. If, for you, that means nothing less than Roederer Cristal, so be it. But what one really needs is a sparkling wine good enough to raise a smile at a price that will not inhibit its frequent use. It should always be ready—that is, chilled. The soft pop of the cork and the delicate foam of a sparkling wine never fail to strike an immediate and appropriate note of gaiety and intimacy. Even the most exquisite still white wine doesn't have that effect. In fact, the finer the white wine, the more serious one's guests feel obliged to be, to show appreciation. There are plenty of well-made, dry, Champagne-method sparkling wines from all over at well under ten dollars a bottle. As an opening for any social occasion, however informal, a sparkling wine always succeeds.

When I'm alone or enjoying a quiet hour with just one or two others, I like a few freshly toasted almonds with a chilled, bone-dry, but properly aged *fino* Sherry. If the *fino* is chosen carefully—three of the best are Valdespino's Ynocente, Domecq's La Ina, and La Guita, a Manzanilla aged near the sea at Sanlúcar de Barrameda and less widely distributed than the other two—even those who respond with doubt when Sherry is mentioned are converted by its aroma and flavor. I always keep a bottle of Ynocente or La Guita in the refrigerator door, and a replacement bottle or two ready in the cellar. In summer, as a substitute for the Sherry,

I sometimes—and only before lunch, never in the evening—switch to a dry white vermouth. Boissière has a flavor I find particularly appealing, and I pour it with a splash of club soda, a couple of ice cubes, and a slice of lemon. As an aperitif it's light and refreshing, and, for many, a slightly exotic change from a glass of white wine.

For the table it's useful to have at least one white wine with texture—silky, firm—and a flavor so modulated that it doesn't become obtrusive or tedious. A discreet California Chardonnay without oakiness or exaggerated fruit serves well. So does a good Mâcon, a Rully, a Montagny, or a white Mercurey from Burgundy. Soave, Orvieto, and Pinot Grigio from the Adige valley can also remain companionable even when used frequently.

Whites consumed regularly should be fresh—so supplies need never exceed what might be drunk over a month or so. In any case, it's best to pick no more than two or three white wines for the cellar at a given time, changing any that pall for something else when next stocking up. If the selection is too broad, confusion reigns, making it impossible to notice how individual wines change in different circumstances and with different foods. The importance of familiarity with a wine is that this enables you to understand it and appreciate all it offers.

As far as red wines are concerned, some people like light, fruity, quaffing wines—Beaujolais, Bourgueil, Valpolicella, wines from the Côte Chalonnaise, California's simpler Zinfandels—and others prefer weightier, bigger-flavored wines they can almost chew: Rhône wines from Gigondas and Vacqueyras, Barberas from Piemonte, Rioja Reservas, offbeat Italian reds like Taurino from Salice Salentino, and Zinfandels from Paso Robles and the Sierra foothills. Barring an unshakably exclusive preference for one or the other, there should be room in a wine cellar for both as well as a few that strike a balance between them. These might include youngish wine from the lower Médoc or from Bourg, across the Gironde, for example; Merlots from Washington State; reds from Corbières in the French southwest; or

Cabernet Sauvignons now on the market from vineyards planted within the last ten years around Lodi, east of San Francisco. (Mondavi's Woodbridge, Sebastiani's Country Varietals, and Cook's California Varietals are largely Lodi grown.)

It's in choosing the wines to be laid away for special occasions that one is most likely to heed (or at least read) the critics and try to draw conclusions from their sometimes conflicting opinions. Don't take them too seriously. Over time, familiarity with the standards and styles of growers whose wines appeal to you will be a much better guide than the opinions of others. There is real satisfaction in getting to know the wine from a particular producer or vineyard as expressed in successive vintages. One learns to take pleasure in recognizing how the grower adapts to each year's imperatives while protecting the inherent characteristics of his wine. That deeper insight is much more gratifying than playing hopscotch around the classed growths, hoping to land on someone else's idea of this year's "best."

It would be presumptuous of me to propose one wine rather than another for this particular category—this is where one should indulge a personal curiosity and allow the occasional extravagance in the pursuit of happiness. Bordeaux wines, great Burgundies, and California Cabernet Sauvignons from the state's most serious producers are sure to be represented. I would like to suggest only that no one be so starstruck by the great wines of Bordeaux as to overlook the thrill in discovering some of the good bourgeois growths, such as Chasse-Spleen, Poujeaux, Monbrison, and Sociando-Mallet; so dazzled by Bordeaux at large that the rest of France is ignored; or so overwhelmed by France in general that wines like Spain's Ribera del Duero and Italy's Barbaresco slip by. To start a cellar, after all, is to embark on an adventure with no particular destination in mind but with unimagined possibilities of distraction along the way. The journey is likely to be sensational.

*—Gerald Asher*

# KEEPING A CELLAR RECORD

George Saintsbury's *Notes On A Cellar Book,* published in 1920, is still one of the most successful wine books in English. It ran to three editions in its first year and has been reprinted often ever since. Though no more than a short collection of reminiscence and commentary provoked by a perusal of the cellar records he had kept for most of his life, *Notes On A Cellar Book* so captured the essence of the man (and the imagination of his readers) that it eclipsed Saintsbury's entire, voluminous, and distinguished body of work published both before and during his tenure as Professor of Rhetoric and English Literature at the University of Edinburgh. As Saintsbury found, a record of what one drank—when, why, with what, and with whom—offers a richer and more revealing vein of personal history than a schedule of diary appointments.

The pages of this *Wine Journal* dedicated to cellar records have been designed to encourage George Saintsbury's successors to note down all the information they'll need, not only for successful reminiscing, but also for keeping track of the wines they have purchased and consumed over the years. There is space to note the wine's complete identity: its appellation, the name of the vineyard or estate (if given), and the name of the grower. If bottled by a merchant, his name can be recorded. Every particular, after all, can be relevant—is the wine a Riserva or an Auslese? was it domain- or chateau-bottled? Sometimes there's useful information on the back label. The actual labels, glued to the page, or hinged on it with a strip of adhesive tape, were once key exhibits of every cellar record. Unfortunately, soaking them off the old-fashioned way now rarely works. New coatings that help bottles slip past one another without breaking on high-speed bottling lines have obliged producers to use adhesives so powerful that the only way to detach most labels is with a product certain to destroy them. Even small growers who bottle by hand are obliged to use the same coated bottles and are therefore unable to avoid these new high-tech glues.

It will be important later to remember what prompted the purchase of a particular wine. Was it recommended in an article, a newsletter, an advertisement, or by word of mouth? Write down what you were told about the wine and its potential development. If you tasted the wine yourself before buying it, copy your original tasting note into the book as a benchmark.

Every time a bottle of the wine is opened, write down where that was, and when. Note down the food eaten with it, and the names of those who were with you. Don't worry about professional jargon. Give your thoughts on the wine in straightforward language that will be as clear to a grandson or granddaughter reading your comment fifty years from now as it is to you. Compare what you find in the wine with what you expected from it, given your initial tasting or the recommendation that led you to buy it. As time goes by, compare the wine with your appreciation of it on previous occasions. Is it still as lively? Is the color unchanged? Has the bouquet intensified or is it fading? Is the wine as smooth as it was, or has it started to dry out? Does it seem to finish with a rasp when it didn't before? Should it be drunk up?

It is amazing how easily we can write about a wine without saying, unequivocally, whether or not we like it. Make a note of what your guests thought. There is no need to rate a wine with a score—as there is no absolute in taste, numbers are meaningless anyway. But you might like to record whether you found the wine poor, average, or good, and even make finer gradations (below average, very good, excellent) if you feel so inclined. As you look through your cellar records in later years, you will see how each each wine evolved over time, and how your own tastes and preferences evolved, too. As far as any individual wine is concerned, you'll recognize the point at which you seemed most to like a wine and the moment when it began to lose its appeal. You'll see which foods brought out the best in it, and which didn't. You'll be reminded of how many bottles were opened with whom, and whose taste most coincided with your own. Above all, you will find that the record will eventually revive memories of more than the wine and the food and who was there to share them.

Wine: _MARIAGE - PINOT NOIR_
_Sonoma County_

Producer: _MARTIN ERAY_          Vintage: _2001_

Quantity purchased: _1 BOI_          Date: _9-12-05_

Price: _$10.50_

Acquired from: _COSTCO_

Original tasting note or recommendation report: _Smooth, clean_
_finish, nice after taste_

Storage location:

## USAGE

~ Date:                    Number of bottles:                    Stock balance:

Served with:

Guests:

Comments:


~ Date:                    Number of bottles:                    Stock balance:

Served with:

Guests:

Comments:


~ Date:                    Number of bottles:                    Stock balance:

Served with:

Guests:

Comments:

# CELLAR RECORD

Wine: *Pinot Noir*

Producer: *Winery Exchange - Oregon* *Newburg,* Vintage: *2004*

Quantity purchased: *1* Date: *4/26/06*

Price:

Acquired from: *Costco*

Original tasting note or recommendation report: *Fruity but light Excellent!*

Storage location:

USAGE

~ Date:      Number of bottles:      Stock balance:

Served with: *Pinot*

Guests:

Comments:


~ Date:      Number of bottles:      Stock balance:

Served with:

Guests:

Comments:


~ Date:      Number of bottles:      Stock balance:

Served with:

Guests:

Comments:

Wine: CARMENERE, CHILE
APALTAGNA

Producer:                                    Vintage:

Quantity purchased:      /              Date:

Price: 18.

Acquired from:

Original tasting note or recommendation report: GOOD SMOOTH
RED, INTERESTING FINISH

Storage location:

## USAGE

~ Date:                Number of bottles:            Stock balance:

Served with: Cheese - Bubo ICK/

Guests:                                Pinot Grigio

Comments:                    Tasted Watery

~ Date:                Number of bottles:            Stock balance:

Served with:

Guests:

Comments:

~ Date:                Number of bottles:            Stock balance:

Served with:

Guests:

Comments:

Wine: *Gargonega, Gini, Soave Classico 2006*

Producer:                           Vintage:

Quantity purchased: *Good!*     Date:

Price:

Acquired from:

Original tasting note or recommendation report:

Storage location:

USAGE

~ Date: *11 2008*   Number of bottles: *2*   Stock balance:

Served with: *Pasta*

Guests:

Comments:

~ Date:            Number of bottles:       Stock balance:

Served with:

Guests:

Comments:

~ Date:            Number of bottles:       Stock balance:

Served with:

Guests:

Comments:

Wine: *Trevor Jones - Australian unoaked Chardonney*

Producer:                 Vintage:

Quantity purchased: *Excellent*     Date:

Price:

Acquired from: *Tried at Roup in SF*

Original tasting note or recommendation report:

Storage location:

USAGE

~ Date:        Number of bottles:       Stock balance:

Served with:

Guests:

Comments:

~ Date:        Number of bottles:       Stock balance:

Served with:

Guests:

Comments:

~ Date:        Number of bottles:       Stock balance:

Served with:

Guests:

Comments:

Wine: **Challis Lane – Chardonnay 2007 Chardonnay**

Producer:      Vintage: **2007**

Quantity purchased: **2**      Date: **1/2008**

Price: **5.00**

Acquired from: **Bev + More**

Original tasting note or recommendation report: **Creamy, nice finish, great price, very good!**

Storage location:

USAGE

~ Date:      Number of bottles:      Stock balance:

Served with:

Guests:

Comments:

~ Date:      Number of bottles:      Stock balance:

Served with:

Guests:

Comments:

~ Date:      Number of bottles:      Stock balance:

Served with:

Guests:

Comments:

Wine: **Pinot Grigio**

Producer: **F F Coppola**  Vintage: **2006**

Quantity purchased:  Date: **8-8-08**

Price:

Acquired from:

Original tasting note or recommendation report: **Pear, apple**

**Crisp, refreshing — Excellent Grigio!**

Storage location:

## USAGE

~ Date: **3/11**  Number of bottles:  Stock balance:

Served with:

Guests:

Comments:

~ Date:  Number of bottles:  Stock balance:

Served with:

Guests:

Comments:

~ Date:  Number of bottles:  Stock balance:

Served with:

Guests:

Comments:

# CELLAR RECORD

Wine:

Producer:                                    Vintage:

Quantity purchased:                          Date:

Price:

Acquired from:

Original tasting note or recommendation report:

Storage location:

USAGE

~ Date:              Number of bottles:      Stock balance:

Served with:

Guests:

Comments:

~ Date:              Number of bottles:      Stock balance:

Served with:

Guests:

Comments:

~ Date:              Number of bottles:      Stock balance:

Served with:

Guests:

Comments:

# CELLAR RECORD

Wine: *Murphy - Goode - 3/11*
*Chardonnay*

Producer:                                    Vintage:

Quantity purchased: *2*              Date: *2008*

Price: *$10 -*

Acquired from:

Original tasting note or recommendation report:
*Fair but worth $10 -*
*I would buy more -*

Storage location:

## USAGE

~ Date:              Number of bottles:              Stock balance:

Served with: *Lasagna*

Guests:

Comments:


~ Date:              Number of bottles:              Stock balance:

Served with:

Guests:

Comments:


~ Date:              Number of bottles:              Stock balance:

Served with:

Guests:

Comments:

# CELLAR RECORD

Wine:

Producer:          Vintage:

Quantity purchased:          Date:

Price:

Acquired from:

Original tasting note or recommendation report:

Storage location:

## USAGE

~ Date:          Number of bottles:          Stock balance:

Served with:

Guests:

Comments:

~ Date:          Number of bottles:          Stock balance:

Served with:

Guests:

Comments:

~ Date:          Number of bottles:          Stock balance:

Served with:

Guests:

Comments:

Wine: Condesa de Sarabella Cosecha - Red Wine

Producer:                                  Vintage: 2004

Quantity purchased: -1-              Date: 8-23-05

Price:

Acquired from:

Original tasting note or recommendation report: Dry

Storage location:

USAGE

~ Date:           Number of bottles:       Stock balance:

Served with:

Guests:

Comments:

~ Date:           Number of bottles:       Stock balance:

Served with:

Guests:

Comments:

~ Date:           Number of bottles:       Stock balance:

Served with:

Guests:

Comments:

☆

Wine: Vouvray - Marie Beauregard
Saget La Perrière

Producer:

Vintage: 2015

Quantity purchased:

Date: 4-17

Price:

Acquired from:

Original tasting note or recommendation report:

Storage location:

USAGE

~ Date: Number of bottles: Stock balance:

Served with:

Guests:

Comments:

~ Date: Number of bottles: Stock balance:

Served with:

Guests:

Comments:

~ Date: Number of bottles: Stock balance:

Served with:

Guests:

Comments:

# CELLAR RECORD

Wine: *Pinot Noir*

Producer: *David Bruce*     Vintage: *2003*

Quantity purchased: *- 1 -*     Date: *7/10/05*

Price: *11.99*

Acquired from: *Costco*

Original tasting note or recommendation report: *Smooth, fruity, excellent*

*Score: 9*

Storage location: *Room Temperature*

## USAGE

~ Date: *8-23-05*    Number of bottles:    Stock balance:

Served with:

Guests:

Comments:

~ Date:    Number of bottles:    Stock balance:

Served with:

Guests:

Comments:

~ Date:    Number of bottles:    Stock balance:

Served with:

Guests:

Comments:

Wine: **Gina - St. Helena**

Producer: **Flora Springs Winery**   Vintage: **2003**

Quantity purchased: **-1-**   Date: **2003 7/20/05**

Price: **6.99**

Acquired from: **Beverges & More**

Original tasting note or recommendation report: **Dry, pears, clean finish, no bougut. Next day, improved. Score: 5   tast and quality. Score: 7**

Storage location: **Refrigerator**

## USAGE

~ Date: **4**   Number of bottles:   Stock balance:

Served with:

Guests:

Comments:

~ Date:   Number of bottles:   Stock balance:

Served with:

Guests:

Comments:

~ Date:   Number of bottles:   Stock balance:

Served with:

Guests:

Comments:

# CELLAR RECORD

Wine:

Producer:                                          Vintage:

Quantity purchased:                                Date:

Price:

Acquired from:

Original tasting note or recommendation report:

Storage location:

## USAGE

~ Date:                    Number of bottles:      Stock balance:

Served with:

Guests:

Comments:

~ Date:                    Number of bottles:      Stock balance:

Served with:

Guests:

Comments:

~ Date:                    Number of bottles:      Stock balance:

Served with:

Guests:

Comments:

Wine: Sauvignon Blank

Producer: Buena Vista      Vintage: 2003

Quantity purchased: -1-      Date: 8-29-05

Price:

Acquired from:

Original tasting note or recommendation report: Clear & crisp, not too sweet

Storage location:

USAGE

~ Date:      Number of bottles:      Stock balance:

Served with:

Guests:

Comments:

~ Date:      Number of bottles:      Stock balance:

Served with:

Guests:

Comments:

~ Date:      Number of bottles:      Stock balance:

Served with:

Guests:

Comments:

# CELLAR RECORD

Wine:

Producer:                                    Vintage:

Quantity purchased:                          Date:

Price:

Acquired from:

Original tasting note or recommendation report:


Storage location:

## USAGE

~ Date:              Number of bottles:      Stock balance:

Served with:

Guests:

Comments:


~ Date:              Number of bottles:      Stock balance:

Served with:

Guests:

Comments:


~ Date:              Number of bottles:      Stock balance:

Served with:

Guests:

Comments:

Wine: *Rodney Strong - 2003 Chalk Hill Chardonnay*

Producer:                                                   Vintage:

Quantity purchased: *1*                Date: *4-20-06*

Price: *$12*

Acquired from: *Beverages + More*

Original tasting note or recommendation report: *Excellent - Smooth + Crisp*

Storage location:

USAGE

~ Date:              Number of bottles:        Stock balance:

Served with:

Guests:

Comments:

~ Date:              Number of bottles:        Stock balance:

Served with:

Guests:

Comments:

~ Date:              Number of bottles:        Stock balance:

Served with:

Guests:

Comments:

# CELLAR RECORD

Wine:

Producer:                                          Vintage:

Quantity purchased:                                Date:

Price:

Acquired from:

Original tasting note or recommendation report:



Storage location:

USAGE

~ Date:              Number of bottles:           Stock balance:

Served with:

Guests:

Comments:



~ Date:              Number of bottles:           Stock balance:

Served with:

Guests:

Comments:



~ Date:              Number of bottles:           Stock balance:

Served with:

Guests:

Comments:

Wine: *Pinot Noir*

Producer: *Tower Brook*  Vintage: *2007*

Quantity purchased:  Date:

Price:

Acquired from: *Prima*

Original tasting note or recommendation report:

Storage location:

USAGE

~ Date:  Number of bottles:  Stock balance:

Served with:

Guests:

Comments:

~ Date:  Number of bottles:  Stock balance:

Served with:

Guests:

Comments:

~ Date:  Number of bottles:  Stock balance:

Served with:

Guests:

Comments:

*Organic* CELLAR RECORD *Whites*

Wine: Bon Terra Vineyards ✳

Producer: Mendecino Vintage:

Quantity purchased: Date:

Price:

Acquired from: Scale of 1 - 10 = 6

Original tasting note or recommendation report: Creamy

Storage location:

USAGE

~ Date: Number of bottles: Stock balance:

Served with:

Guests:

Comments:

~ Date: Number of bottles: Stock balance:

Served with:

Guests:

Comments:

~ Date: Number of bottles: Stock balance:

Served with:

Guests:

Comments:

# CELLAR RECORD

Wine: *Heitz Cellar*

*Excellent*

Producer: _____ Vintage: _____

Quantity purchased: _____ Date: _____

Price: _____

Acquired from: _____

Original tasting note or recommendation report:

_____

_____

Storage location: _____

## USAGE

~ Date: _____ Number of bottles: _____ Stock balance: _____

Served with: _____

Guests: _____

Comments: _____

_____

~ Date: _____ Number of bottles: _____ Stock balance: _____

Served with: _____

Guests: _____

Comments: _____

_____

~ Date: _____ Number of bottles: _____ Stock balance: _____

Served with: _____

Guests: _____

Comments: _____

_____

Wine: Solitude Wines

Producer: Pinot Noir     Vintage: 2007

Quantity purchased:     Date:

Price:

Acquired from: Prima Winery

Original tasting note or recommendation report:

~~An~~ Organic

Storage location: Excellent

## USAGE

~ Date:     Number of bottles:     Stock balance:

Served with:

Guests:

Comments:


~ Date:     Number of bottles:     Stock balance:

Served with:

Guests:

Comments:


~ Date:     Number of bottles:     Stock balance:

Served with:

Guests:

Comments:

Wine: *Pinot Noir - BEST Pinot or wine I ever*

Producer: *Emeritis*    Vintage: *tested*

Quantity purchased:    Date:

Price:

Acquired from:

Original tasting note or recommendation report: *Unbelievable! Very smooth, great finish & bouquet*

Storage location:

USAGE

~ Date:    Number of bottles:    Stock balance:

Served with:

Guests:

Comments:

~ Date:    Number of bottles:    Stock balance:

Served with:

Guests:

Comments:

~ Date:    Number of bottles:    Stock balance:

Served with:

Guests:

Comments:

# CELLAR RECORD

Wine: *Morgan Chardonay + Pinot Gris - 2009*

Producer: *Morgan* *Very nice!* Vintage:

Quantity purchased: Date:

Price:

Acquired from:

Original tasting note or recommendation report:

Storage location:

USAGE

~ Date:               Number of bottles:          Stock balance:

Served with:

Guests:

Comments:

~ Date:               Number of bottles:          Stock balance:

Served with:

Guests:

Comments:

~ Date:               Number of bottles:          Stock balance:

Served with:

Guests:

Comments:

# CELLAR RECORD

Wine: *Carneros Creek Reserve*

Producer: Vintage: *Chardonay*

Quantity purchased: *2012* Date:

Price:

Acquired from: *Excellent !*

Original tasting note or recommendation report:

Storage location:

USAGE

~ Date: Number of bottles: Stock balance:

Served with:

Guests:

Comments:

~ Date: Number of bottles: Stock balance:

Served with:

Guests:

Comments:

~ Date: Number of bottles: Stock balance:

Served with:

Guests:

Comments:

# CELLAR RECORD

Wine: Gloria Ferrer

Producer: Carneros                    Vintage: 2008
Quantity purchased:                    Date: 8/2011
Price: Chardonay
Acquired from:                         (8)
Original tasting note or recommendation report: Not creamy, but more fruity & smooth. Very good for price
Storage location:

USAGE

~ Date:              Number of bottles:        Stock balance:
Served with:
Guests:
Comments:


~ Date:              Number of bottles:        Stock balance:
Served with:
Guests:
Comments:


~ Date:              Number of bottles:        Stock balance:
Served with:
Guests:
Comments:

# CELLAR RECORD

Wine: *Siduri – Costco*

Producer: *Pinot Noir*   Vintage:

Quantity purchased: *2013*   Date:

Price:

Acquired from: *Smooth*

Original tasting note or recommendation report:

Storage location:

USAGE

~ Date:                Number of bottles:              Stock balance:

Served with:

Guests:

Comments:

~ Date:                Number of bottles:              Stock balance:

Served with:

Guests:

Comments:

~ Date:                Number of bottles:              Stock balance:

Served with:

Guests:

Comments:

# CELLAR RECORD

Wine:

Producer:                                    Vintage:

Quantity purchased:                          Date:

Price:

Acquired from:

Original tasting note or recommendation report:

Storage location:

USAGE

~ Date:                Number of bottles:        Stock balance:

Served with:

Guests:

Comments:

~ Date:                Number of bottles:        Stock balance:

Served with:

Guests:

Comments:

~ Date:                Number of bottles:        Stock balance:

Served with:

Guests:

Comments:

# CELLAR RECORD

Wine:

Producer:                              Vintage:

Quantity purchased:                    Date:

Price:

Acquired from:

Original tasting note or recommendation report:

Storage location:

## USAGE

~ Date:              Number of bottles:        Stock balance:

Served with:

Guests:

Comments:

~ Date:              Number of bottles:        Stock balance:

Served with:

Guests:

Comments:

~ Date:              Number of bottles:        Stock balance:

Served with:

Guests:

Comments:

# CELLAR RECORD

Wine:

Producer:                                    Vintage:

Quantity purchased:                          Date:

Price:

Acquired from:

Original tasting note or recommendation report:

Storage location:

USAGE

~ Date:              Number of bottles:       Stock balance:

Served with:

Guests:

Comments:

~ Date:              Number of bottles:       Stock balance:

Served with:

Guests:

Comments:

~ Date:              Number of bottles:       Stock balance:

Served with:

Guests:

Comments:

Wine:

Producer:                                    Vintage:

Quantity purchased:                          Date:

Price:

Acquired from:

Original tasting note or recommendation report:

Storage location:

USAGE

~ Date:              Number of bottles:        Stock balance:

Served with:

Guests:

Comments:

~ Date:              Number of bottles:        Stock balance:

Served with:

Guests:

Comments:

~ Date:              Number of bottles:        Stock balance:

Served with:

Guests:

Comments:

Wine:

Producer:                                    Vintage:

Quantity purchased:                          Date:

Price:

Acquired from:

Original tasting note or recommendation report:


Storage location:

## USAGE

~ Date:              Number of bottles:        Stock balance:

Served with:

Guests:

Comments:


~ Date:              Number of bottles:        Stock balance:

Served with:

Guests:

Comments:


~ Date:              Number of bottles:        Stock balance:

Served with:

Guests:

Comments:

Wine:

Producer:          Vintage:

Quantity purchased:        Date:

Price:

Acquired from:

Original tasting note or recommendation report:

Storage location:

## USAGE

~ Date:      Number of bottles:      Stock balance:

Served with:

Guests:

Comments:

~ Date:      Number of bottles:      Stock balance:

Served with:

Guests:

Comments:

~ Date:      Number of bottles:      Stock balance:

Served with:

Guests:

Comments:

Wine:

Producer:                                    Vintage:

Quantity purchased:                          Date:

Price:

Acquired from:

Original tasting note or recommendation report:

Storage location:

USAGE

~ Date:              Number of bottles:        Stock balance:

Served with:

Guests:

Comments:

~ Date:              Number of bottles:        Stock balance:

Served with:

Guests:

Comments:

~ Date:              Number of bottles:        Stock balance:

Served with:

Guests:

Comments:

# CELLAR RECORD

Wine:

Producer:                                    Vintage:

Quantity purchased:                          Date:

Price:

Acquired from:

Original tasting note or recommendation report:


Storage location:

## USAGE

~ Date:               Number of bottles:      Stock balance:

Served with:

Guests:

Comments:


~ Date:               Number of bottles:      Stock balance:

Served with:

Guests:

Comments:


~ Date:               Number of bottles:      Stock balance:

Served with:

Guests:

Comments:

Wine:

Producer:                                        Vintage:

Quantity purchased:                              Date:

Price:

Acquired from:

Original tasting note or recommendation report:

Storage location:

USAGE

~ Date:                Number of bottles:        Stock balance:

Served with:

Guests:

Comments:

~ Date:                Number of bottles:        Stock balance:

Served with:

Guests:

Comments:

~ Date:                Number of bottles:        Stock balance:

Served with:

Guests:

Comments:

# CELLAR RECORD

Wine:

Producer:                                                 Vintage:

Quantity purchased:                     Date:

Price:

Acquired from:

Original tasting note or recommendation report:

Storage location:

USAGE

~ Date:                Number of bottles:            Stock balance:

Served with:

Guests:

Comments:

~ Date:                Number of bottles:            Stock balance:

Served with:

Guests:

Comments:

~ Date:                Number of bottles:            Stock balance:

Served with:

Guests:

Comments:

Wine:

Producer:                                          Vintage:

Quantity purchased:                                Date:

Price:

Acquired from:

Original tasting note or recommendation report:

Storage location:

USAGE

~ Date:                    Number of bottles:        Stock balance:

Served with:

Guests:

Comments:

~ Date:                    Number of bottles:        Stock balance:

Served with:

Guests:

Comments:

~ Date:                    Number of bottles:        Stock balance:

Served with:

Guests:

Comments:

Wine:

Producer:                          Vintage:

Quantity purchased:            Date:

Price:

Acquired from:

Original tasting note or recommendation report:

Storage location:

USAGE

~ Date:               Number of bottles:        Stock balance:

Served with:

Guests:

Comments:

~ Date:               Number of bottles:        Stock balance:

Served with:

Guests:

Comments:

~ Date:               Number of bottles:        Stock balance:

Served with:

Guests:

Comments:

# CELLAR RECORD

Wine:

Producer:                                    Vintage:

Quantity purchased:                          Date:

Price:

Acquired from:

Original tasting note or recommendation report:

Storage location:

## USAGE

~ Date:            Number of bottles:        Stock balance:

Served with:

Guests:

Comments:

~ Date:            Number of bottles:        Stock balance:

Served with:

Guests:

Comments:

~ Date:            Number of bottles:        Stock balance:

Served with:

Guests:

Comments:

Wine:

Producer:                                          Vintage:

Quantity purchased:                                Date:

Price:

Acquired from:

Original tasting note or recommendation report:


Storage location:

USAGE

~ Date:                 Number of bottles:        Stock balance:

Served with:

Guests:

Comments:


~ Date:                 Number of bottles:        Stock balance:

Served with:

Guests:

Comments:


~ Date:                 Number of bottles:        Stock balance:

Served with:

Guests:

Comments:

Wine:

Producer:                                             Vintage:

Quantity purchased:                                   Date:

Price:

Acquired from:

Original tasting note or recommendation report:


Storage location:

## USAGE

~ Date:                 Number of bottles:            Stock balance:

Served with:

Guests:

Comments:


~ Date:                 Number of bottles:            Stock balance:

Served with:

Guests:

Comments:


~ Date:                 Number of bottles:            Stock balance:

Served with:

Guests:

Comments:

# CELLAR RECORD

Wine:

Producer:                                       Vintage:

Quantity purchased:                      Date:

Price:

Acquired from:

Original tasting note or recommendation report:

Storage location:

## USAGE

~ Date:                   Number of bottles:             Stock balance:

Served with:

Guests:

Comments:

~ Date:                   Number of bottles:             Stock balance:

Served with:

Guests:

Comments:

~ Date:                   Number of bottles:             Stock balance:

Served with:

Guests:

Comments:

Wine: *Migration* 2010
*Chardonnay*

Producer: *Russian River*    Vintage:

Quantity purchased:    Date:

Price: *Gift*

Acquired from: *Creamy - Excellent!*

Original tasting note or recommendation report:

Storage location:

## USAGE

~ Date:     Number of bottles:     Stock balance:

Served with:

Guests:

Comments:

~ Date:     Number of bottles:     Stock balance:

Served with:

Guests:

Comments:

~ Date:     Number of bottles:     Stock balance:

Served with:

Guests:

Comments:

# CELLAR RECORD

Wine: *Mark West* *Good*

Producer: *Pinot Noir* Vintage: *California 2007*

Quantity purchased: Date:

Price:

Acquired from:

Original tasting note or recommendation report:

Storage location:

USAGE

~ Date: Number of bottles: Stock balance:

Served with:

Guests:

Comments:

~ Date: Number of bottles: Stock balance:

Served with:

Guests:

Comments:

~ Date: Number of bottles: Stock balance:

Served with:

Guests:

Comments:

# CELLAR RECORD

Wine:

Producer:                              Vintage:

Quantity purchased:                    Date:

Price:

Acquired from:

Original tasting note or recommendation report:


Storage location:

USAGE

~ Date:            Number of bottles:        Stock balance:

Served with:

Guests:

Comments:


~ Date:            Number of bottles:        Stock balance:

Served with:

Guests:

Comments:


~ Date:            Number of bottles:        Stock balance:

Served with:

Guests:

Comments:

# CELLAR RECORD

Wine:

Producer:                  Vintage:

Quantity purchased:          Date:

Price:

Acquired from:

Original tasting note or recommendation report:

Storage location:

## USAGE

~ Date:        Number of bottles:        Stock balance:

Served with:

Guests:

Comments:

~ Date:        Number of bottles:        Stock balance:

Served with:

Guests:

Comments:

~ Date:        Number of bottles:        Stock balance:

Served with:

Guests:

Comments:

Wine: *The Novelist*

Producer: 2015 White Vintage:

Quantity purchased: Date:

Price: *Creamy*

Acquired from:

Original tasting note or recommendation report:

Storage location:

USAGE

~ Date:      Number of bottles:      Stock balance:

Served with:

Guests:

Comments:

~ Date:      Number of bottles:      Stock balance:

Served with:

Guests:

Comments:

~ Date:      Number of bottles:      Stock balance:

Served with:

Guests:

Comments:

# CELLAR RECORD

Wine:

Producer:                                    Vintage:

Quantity purchased:                          Date:

Price:

Acquired from:

Original tasting note or recommendation report:

Storage location:

## USAGE

~ Date:              Number of bottles:        Stock balance:

Served with:

Guests:

Comments:

~ Date:              Number of bottles:        Stock balance:

Served with:

Guests:

Comments:

~ Date:              Number of bottles:        Stock balance:

Served with:

Guests:

Comments:

# CELLAR RECORD

Wine: Cynthus – Chardonnay 2004
Oliver Lane

Producer: Russian River          Vintage:

Quantity purchased:              Date:

Price: Fair          Good

Acquired from:

Original tasting note or recommendation report:

Storage location:

USAGE

~ Date:          Number of bottles:          Stock balance:

Served with:

Guests:

Comments:

~ Date:          Number of bottles:          Stock balance:

Served with:

Guests:

Comments:

~ Date:          Number of bottles:          Stock balance:

Served with:

Guests:

Comments:

# CELLAR RECORD

Wine:

Producer:                                          Vintage:

Quantity purchased:                                Date:

Price:

Acquired from:

Original tasting note or recommendation report:

Storage location:

USAGE

~ Date:                    Number of bottles:              Stock balance:

Served with:

Guests:

Comments:

~ Date:                    Number of bottles:              Stock balance:

Served with:

Guests:

Comments:

~ Date:                    Number of bottles:              Stock balance:

Served with:

Guests:

Comments:

Wine:

Producer:                                          Vintage:

Quantity purchased:                                Date:

Price:

Acquired from:

Original tasting note or recommendation report:

Storage location:

USAGE

~ Date:              Number of bottles:            Stock balance:

Served with:

Guests:

Comments:

~ Date:              Number of bottles:            Stock balance:

Served with:

Guests:

Comments:

~ Date:              Number of bottles:            Stock balance:

Served with:

Guests:

Comments:

# CELLAR RECORD

Wine:

Producer:                                          Vintage:

Quantity purchased:                                Date:

Price:

Acquired from:

Original tasting note or recommendation report:

Storage location:

## USAGE

~ Date:                    Number of bottles:      Stock balance:

Served with:

Guests:

Comments:

~ Date:                    Number of bottles:      Stock balance:

Served with:

Guests:

Comments:

~ Date:                    Number of bottles:      Stock balance:

Served with:

Guests:

Comments:

# CELLAR RECORD

Wine:

Producer:                                        Vintage:

Quantity purchased:                              Date:

Price:

Acquired from:

Original tasting note or recommendation report:


Storage location:

## USAGE

~ Date:              Number of bottles:          Stock balance:

Served with:

Guests:

Comments:


~ Date:              Number of bottles:          Stock balance:

Served with:

Guests:

Comments:


~ Date:              Number of bottles:          Stock balance:

Served with:

Guests:

Comments:

# CELLAR RECORD

Wine:

Producer:                                    Vintage:

Quantity purchased:                          Date:

Price:

Acquired from:

Original tasting note or recommendation report:


Storage location:

## USAGE

~ Date:              Number of bottles:       Stock balance:

Served with:

Guests:

Comments:


~ Date:              Number of bottles:       Stock balance:

Served with:

Guests:

Comments:


~ Date:              Number of bottles:       Stock balance:

Served with:

Guests:

Comments:

# CELLAR RECORD

Wine:

Producer:                                              Vintage:

Quantity purchased:                              Date:

Price:

Acquired from:

Original tasting note or recommendation report:

Storage location:

USAGE

~ Date:                    Number of bottles:              Stock balance:

Served with:

Guests:

Comments:

~ Date:                    Number of bottles:              Stock balance:

Served with:

Guests:

Comments:

~ Date:                    Number of bottles:              Stock balance:

Served with:

Guests:

Comments:

# CELLAR RECORD

Wine:

Producer:                                          Vintage:

Quantity purchased:                                Date:

Price:

Acquired from:

Original tasting note or recommendation report:

Storage location:

USAGE

~ Date:                 Number of bottles:         Stock balance:

Served with:

Guests:

Comments:

~ Date:                 Number of bottles:         Stock balance:

Served with:

Guests:

Comments:

~ Date:                 Number of bottles:         Stock balance:

Served with:

Guests:

Comments:

# CELLAR RECORD

Wine:

Producer:                                      Vintage:

Quantity purchased:                            Date:

Price:

Acquired from:

Original tasting note or recommendation report:

Storage location:

## USAGE

~ Date:               Number of bottles:        Stock balance:

Served with:

Guests:

Comments:

~ Date:               Number of bottles:        Stock balance:

Served with:

Guests:

Comments:

~ Date:               Number of bottles:        Stock balance:

Served with:

Guests:

Comments:

# CELLAR RECORD

Wine:

Producer:                         Vintage:

Quantity purchased:         Date:

Price:

Acquired from:

Original tasting note or recommendation report:

Storage location:

USAGE

~ Date:           Number of bottles:       Stock balance:

Served with:

Guests:

Comments:

~ Date:           Number of bottles:       Stock balance:

Served with:

Guests:

Comments:

~ Date:           Number of bottles:       Stock balance:

Served with:

Guests:

Comments:

# CELLAR RECORD

Wine:

Producer:                                    Vintage:

Quantity purchased:                          Date:

Price:

Acquired from:

Original tasting note or recommendation report:


Storage location:

## USAGE

~ Date:                Number of bottles:        Stock balance:

Served with:

Guests:

Comments:


~ Date:                Number of bottles:        Stock balance:

Served with:

Guests:

Comments:


~ Date:                Number of bottles:        Stock balance:

Served with:

Guests:

Comments:

# CELLAR RECORD

Wine:

Producer:                                          Vintage:

Quantity purchased:                                Date:

Price:

Acquired from:

Original tasting note or recommendation report:


Storage location:

## USAGE

~ Date:              Number of bottles:           Stock balance:

Served with:

Guests:

Comments:


~ Date:              Number of bottles:           Stock balance:

Served with:

Guests:

Comments:


~ Date:              Number of bottles:           Stock balance:

Served with:

Guests:

Comments:

Wine:

Producer:                                          Vintage:

Quantity purchased:                        Date:

Price:

Acquired from:

Original tasting note or recommendation report:

Storage location:

USAGE

~ Date:                    Number of bottles:                    Stock balance:

Served with:

Guests:

Comments:

~ Date:                    Number of bottles:                    Stock balance:

Served with:

Guests:

Comments:

~ Date:                    Number of bottles:                    Stock balance:

Served with:

Guests:

Comments:

Wine: _Goyette 2011 — Pinot Costco_

Producer: | Vintage:

Quantity purchased: | Date:

Price: _# 14_

Acquired from: _Nice for price_

Original tasting note or recommendation report:

Storage location:

USAGE

~ Date: | Number of bottles: | Stock balance:

Served with:

Guests:

Comments:

~ Date: | Number of bottles: | Stock balance:

Served with:

Guests:

Comments:

~ Date: | Number of bottles: | Stock balance:

Served with:

Guests:

Comments:

Wine: *Raymond*

Producer:                                   Vintage: *2006*

Quantity purchased:                 Date:

Price:

Acquired from: *Unicorn Restaurant - SF*

Original tasting note or recommendation report:

Storage location:

USAGE

~ Date:            Number of bottles:        Stock balance:

Served with:

Guests:

Comments:

~ Date:            Number of bottles:        Stock balance:

Served with:

Guests:

Comments:

~ Date:            Number of bottles:        Stock balance:

Served with:

Guests:

Comments:

Wine:

Producer:                                              Vintage:

Quantity purchased:                          Date:

Price:

Acquired from:

Original tasting note or recommendation report:

Storage location:

USAGE

~ Date:                    Number of bottles:              Stock balance:

Served with:

Guests:

Comments:

~ Date:                    Number of bottles:              Stock balance:

Served with:

Guests:

Comments:

~ Date:                    Number of bottles:              Stock balance:

Served with:

Guests:

Comments:

# CELLAR RECORD

Wine:

Producer:                                    Vintage:

Quantity purchased:                          Date:

Price:

Acquired from:

Original tasting note or recommendation report:


Storage location:

USAGE

~ Date:              Number of bottles:       Stock balance:

Served with:

Guests:

Comments:


~ Date:              Number of bottles:       Stock balance:

Served with:

Guests:

Comments:


~ Date:              Number of bottles:       Stock balance:

Served with:

Guests:

Comments:

# WRITING A TASTING NOTE

When a wine in a restaurant or at a friend's table makes an impression on us, we think we shall always remember it. But we won't unless we make a note of it. A tasting note is never more than a sketch, and it's therefore more important to emphasize the key details than to bury them in an avalanche of adjectives.

First we need to be sure we have copied down all the label information that will enable us to identify the wine exactly—including the name of the U. S. importer in case we need to ask a wine merchant to trace the wine for our own cellar.

We get three impressions when we taste—sight, smell and taste (which includes touch). In a fine wine, all three flow together harmoniously. From first glimpse to last, lingering impression on the palate, a wine should be seamless. The better the wine, the more difficult it is to analyze.

What we see helps us judge the wine's age and condition. Is it quite clear? Tilt the glass and look at the rim of the wine against a white cloth or counter. If red, is it the purple red of very young wine, or has it progressed to garnet, light ruby, or brick with advancing years? Refraction varies with a wine's acidity: Does this one gleam as light passes through it, or is there rather a soft sheen? To judge the density of color, one must set the glass down and look from above. How clearly does one see the base? Is there, in a white wine, a hint of green? Is it watery pale, the color of new straw, or a reflection of old gold? Is there a suggestion of amber?

Aroma is based on elements from the grape itself and on those that develop during fermentation; it's an attribute of young wine. The use of selected yeast and fermentation at controlled low temperatures encourage the formation of certain aromas in wine—the principal reason that some white wines, intended to be drunk young, are now more fragrant than they once used to be. Aroma is usually fruity, and whether the result of the grape or the fermentation, will often suggest quite specific fruits—berries, for instance, rather than plum or apricot. A smell of vanilla or of smoky wood in a young wine is usually a sign that it has been housed, for a time at least, in newish oak barrels. By itself, that is not necessarily the indication of quality some assume it to be.

Bouquet is the attribute of mature wine. It is formed when a wine's elements have had time to fuse in the bottle, though there is much to suggest that the foundation of bouquet is set while the wine is still in wood. Bouquet should be suggestive, its tissue so subtle that no one strand should be clearly distinguishable from another. A sudden reminder of mushroom or damp woods as the wine's tannins break down is just as quickly lost to a whiff of chocolate if a red wine was made from grapes grown on vines with a particularly warm and sunny exposure; or of hot sealing wax or violets (even ink) in wines made from Cabernet Sauvignon grapes grown on certain types of soil. Alcohol, tannin, and acidity should be in such balance that none particularly intrudes on our attention. When we notice and need to refer to any one of them, it is usually a sign that there is excess of it (or a deficit of another).

Wherever possible, comments should include a note on the mood of the occasion and the opinions of those who tasted the wine with you. They could have affected your perception of the wine, and it is useful to be reminded of that when thinking of the wine later.

Much of our tasting vocabulary (see the Dictionary of Terms on page 120) has come to us from France, but certain words lose their particular associations when translated literally from French into English. Those who base their tasting notes on half-digested French may end up with descriptions that are meaningless. What the French call *goût de terroir*, for example, does not mean *earthy*, a term frequently used in English, any more than *végétal* means that a wine tastes of

vegetables. The English vocabulary developed in wine schools in recent years is intended to ensure that those who need to discuss professionally the smell and taste of a wine can do so in terms that have agreed and defined values, carefully learned and therefore mutually understood. They are not necessarily the most appropriate terms in which to describe one's own reaction to a gloriously exciting red Burgundy. In fact, in writing of a wine, it's best, for later recall, to capture one's reaction to it rather than attempt a detailed analysis. Analysis does not lead to synthesis: The most careful description will never create or recreate in the mind the actual smell and taste of a wine. One has a better chance of recalling a wine, or allowing another to seize an idea of its style and quality, if the memory of it is allowed to hang on what seems at the time to be a telling hook. That's when expressions such as "wet blackberries," or "cigar box," or "prunes" can be useful as a *personal* conduit back to the entire experience. When such an image pops into the mind, write it down, and don't then muddle it with a dozen other references not half so important.

# TASTING NOTES

Wine:

Producer:                                      Vintage:

Imported by:

Where tasted:                                  Date:

Served with:

Clarity, hue, density of color:

Aroma or bouquet:

Taste, texture, balance and harmony:

Other comments:

~ ~ ~ ~ ~ ~ ~ ~ ~ ~ ~ ~ ~ ~ ~ ~ ~ ~ ~ ~ ~

Wine:

Producer:                                      Vintage:

Imported by:

Where tasted:                                  Date:

Served with:

Clarity, hue, density of color:

Aroma or bouquet:

Taste, texture, balance and harmony:

Other comments:

Wine:

Producer:                                    Vintage:

Imported by:

Where tasted:                                Date:

Served with:

Clarity, hue, density of color:

Aroma or bouquet:

Taste, texture, balance and harmony:

Other comments:

~ ~ ~ ~ ~ ~ ~ ~ ~ ~ ~ ~ ~ ~ ~ ~ ~ ~ ~ ~

Wine:

Producer:                                    Vintage:

Imported by:

Where tasted:                                Date:

Served with:

Clarity, hue, density of color:

Aroma or bouquet:

Taste, texture, balance and harmony:

Other comments:

Wine:

Producer:                                    Vintage:

Imported by:

Where tasted:                                Date:

Served with:

Clarity, hue, density of color:

Aroma or bouquet:


Taste, texture, balance and harmony:


Other comments:




~ ~ ~ ~ ~ ~ ~ ~ ~ ~ ~ ~ ~ ~ ~ ~ ~ ~ ~ ~

Wine:

Producer:                                    Vintage:

Imported by:

Where tasted:                                Date:

Served with:

Clarity, hue, density of color:

Aroma or bouquet:


Taste, texture, balance and harmony:


Other comments:

Wine:

Producer:                                    Vintage:

Imported by:

Where tasted:                                Date:

Served with:

Clarity, hue, density of color:

Aroma or bouquet:

Taste, texture, balance and harmony:

Other comments:

~ ~ ~ ~ ~ ~ ~ ~ ~ ~ ~ ~ ~ ~ ~ ~ ~ ~ ~ ~ ~

Wine:

Producer:                                    Vintage:

Imported by:

Where tasted:                                Date:

Served with:

Clarity, hue, density of color:

Aroma or bouquet:

Taste, texture, balance and harmony:

Other comments:

Wine:

Producer:                                          Vintage:

Imported by:

Where tasted:                                      Date:

Served with:

Clarity, hue, density of color:

Aroma or bouquet:

Taste, texture, balance and harmony:

Other comments:

~ ~ ~ ~ ~ ~ ~ ~ ~ ~ ~ ~ ~ ~ ~ ~ ~ ~ ~

Wine:

Producer:                                          Vintage:

Imported by:

Where tasted:                                      Date:

Served with:

Clarity, hue, density of color:

Aroma or bouquet:

Taste, texture, balance and harmony:

Other comments:

Wine:

Producer: Vintage:

Imported by:

Where tasted: Date:

Served with:

Clarity, hue, density of color:

Aroma or bouquet:

Taste, texture, balance and harmony:

Other comments:

~ ~ ~ ~ ~ ~ ~ ~ ~ ~ ~ ~ ~ ~ ~ ~ ~ ~ ~ ~

Wine:

Producer: Vintage:

Imported by:

Where tasted: Date:

Served with:

Clarity, hue, density of color:

Aroma or bouquet:

Taste, texture, balance and harmony:

Other comments:

# TASTING NOTES

Wine:

Producer:                                    Vintage:

Imported by:

Where tasted:                                Date:

Served with:

Clarity, hue, density of color:

Aroma or bouquet:

Taste, texture, balance and harmony:

Other comments:

~ ~ ~ ~ ~ ~ ~ ~ ~ ~ ~ ~ ~ ~ ~ ~ ~ ~ ~ ~ ~

Wine:

Producer:                                    Vintage:

Imported by:

Where tasted:                                Date:

Served with:

Clarity, hue, density of color:

Aroma or bouquet:

Taste, texture, balance and harmony:

Other comments:

Wine: Bernadus 2003 Chardonnay

Producer: Monterey County Vintage: 2003

Imported by:

Where tasted: Date: 6-15-06

Served with:

Clarity, hue, density of color:

Aroma or bouquet:

Taste, texture, balance and harmony: Great for an average priced wine.

Other comments:

~ ~ ~ ~ ~ ~ ~ ~ ~ ~ ~ ~ ~ ~ ~ ~ ~ ~ ~ ~ ~

Wine: Macon - Villages - Chardonnay

Producer: Lois Jalot - Nice Vintage:

Imported by: French

Where tasted: House Date: 2011

Served with:

Clarity, hue, density of color:

Aroma or bouquet: #15 Trader Joes

Taste, texture, balance and harmony:

Other comments: Appellation - Macon - Villages Controlee

# TASTING NOTES

Wine:

Producer: Vintage:

Imported by:

Where tasted: Date:

Served with:

Clarity, hue, density of color:

Aroma or bouquet:

Taste, texture, balance and harmony:

Other comments:

~ ~ ~ ~ ~ ~ ~ ~ ~ ~ ~ ~ ~ ~ ~ ~ ~ ~ ~ ~

Wine:

Producer: Vintage:

Imported by:

Where tasted: Date:

Served with:

Clarity, hue, density of color:

Aroma or bouquet:

Taste, texture, balance and harmony:

Other comments:

# TASTING NOTES

Wine:

Producer: Vintage:

Imported by:

Where tasted: Date:

Served with:

Clarity, hue, density of color:

Aroma or bouquet:

Taste, texture, balance and harmony:

Other comments:

~ ~ ~ ~ ~ ~ ~ ~ ~ ~ ~ ~ ~ ~ ~ ~ ~ ~ ~

Wine:

Producer: Vintage:

Imported by:

Where tasted: Date:

Served with:

Clarity, hue, density of color:

Aroma or bouquet:

Taste, texture, balance and harmony:

Other comments:

Wine:

Producer:                                          Vintage:

Imported by:

Where tasted:                                      Date:

Served with:

Clarity, hue, density of color:

Aroma or bouquet:

Taste, texture, balance and harmony:

Other comments:

~ ~ ~ ~ ~ ~ ~ ~ ~ ~ ~ ~ ~ ~ ~ ~ ~ ~ ~ ~ ~

Wine:

Producer:                                          Vintage:

Imported by:

Where tasted:                                      Date:

Served with:

Clarity, hue, density of color:

Aroma or bouquet:

Taste, texture, balance and harmony:

Other comments:

Wine:

Producer:                                    Vintage:

Imported by:

Where tasted:                                Date:

Served with:

Clarity, hue, density of color:

Aroma or bouquet:

Taste, texture, balance and harmony:

Other comments:

~ ~ ~ ~ ~ ~ ~ ~ ~ ~ ~ ~ ~ ~ ~ ~ ~ ~ ~ ~

Wine:

Producer:                                    Vintage:

Imported by:

Where tasted:                                Date:

Served with:

Clarity, hue, density of color:

Aroma or bouquet:

Taste, texture, balance and harmony:

Other comments:

# TASTING NOTES

Wine:

Producer:                                    Vintage:

Imported by:

Where tasted:                                Date:

Served with:

Clarity, hue, density of color:

Aroma or bouquet:

Taste, texture, balance and harmony:

Other comments:

~ ~ ~ ~ ~ ~ ~ ~ ~ ~ ~ ~ ~ ~ ~ ~ ~ ~ ~ ~

Wine:

Producer:                                    Vintage:

Imported by:

Where tasted:                                Date:

Served with:

Clarity, hue, density of color:

Aroma or bouquet:

Taste, texture, balance and harmony:

Other comments:

Wine:

Producer:                                    Vintage:

Imported by:

Where tasted:                                Date:

Served with:

Clarity, hue, density of color:

Aroma or bouquet:

Taste, texture, balance and harmony:

Other comments:

~ ~ ~ ~ ~ ~ ~ ~ ~ ~ ~ ~ ~ ~ ~ ~ ~ ~ ~ ~ ~

Wine:

Producer:                                    Vintage:

Imported by:

Where tasted:                                Date:

Served with:

Clarity, hue, density of color:

Aroma or bouquet:

Taste, texture, balance and harmony:

Other comments:

Wine: *Selby*  *Excellent!*

Producer: *Zin Bobcat*   Vintage: *2014*

Imported by:

Where tasted:                Date:

Served with:

Clarity, hue, density of color:

Aroma or bouquet:

Taste, texture, balance and harmony:

Other comments: *Healdsburg*

~ ~ ~ ~ ~ ~ ~ ~ ~ ~ ~ ~ ~ ~ ~ ~ ~ ~ ~ ~ ~

Wine:

Producer:                Vintage:

Imported by:

Where tasted:                Date:

Served with:

Clarity, hue, density of color:

Aroma or bouquet:

Taste, texture, balance and harmony:

Other comments:

Wine: *La Puerta Alta Torrontes 2010*

Producer: Vintage:

Imported by: *Famatina Valley*

Where tasted: *Argentina* Date:

Served with:

Clarity, hue, density of color: *Good !*

Aroma or bouquet:

Taste, texture, balance and harmony:

Other comments:

~ ~ ~ ~ ~ ~ ~ ~ ~ ~ ~ ~ ~ ~ ~ ~ ~ ~ ~ ~ ~

Wine:

Producer: Vintage:

Imported by:

Where tasted: Date:

Served with:

Clarity, hue, density of color:

Aroma or bouquet:

Taste, texture, balance and harmony:

Other comments:

Wine: _Quivira — Pig on Bottle_

Producer: _2009_     Vintage:

Imported by: _Zinfandel_

Where tasted:     Date:

Served with: _Great !_

Clarity, hue, density of color: _Great !_   _$15.00_

Aroma or bouquet: _Costco_

Taste, texture, balance and harmony:

Other comments:

~ ~ ~ ~ ~ ~ ~ ~ ~ ~ ~ ~ ~ ~ ~ ~ ~ ~ ~ ~ ~ ~ ~

Wine: _Raymond — 9 - Good_

Producer: _Reserve -_     Vintage:

Imported by: _Sauvignon Blanc_

Where tasted: _2009_     Date:

Served with:

Clarity, hue, density of color:

Aroma or bouquet:

Taste, texture, balance and harmony:

Other comments:

Wine: *Vichon –Chardonnay 2010*

Producer: *1 to 10 a (3)*    Vintage:

Imported by:

Where tasted:    Date:

Served with:

Clarity, hue, density of color:

Aroma or bouquet:

Taste, texture, balance and harmony:

Other comments:

~ ~ ~ ~ ~ ~ ~ ~ ~ ~ ~ ~ ~ ~ ~ ~ ~ ~ ~ ~ ~

Wine:

Producer:    Vintage:

Imported by:

Where tasted:    Date:

Served with:

Clarity, hue, density of color:

Aroma or bouquet:

Taste, texture, balance and harmony:

Other comments:

Wine: *Cheese –* Unie Kaas cheese
Whole Foods – Aged Cheddar

Producer: Excellent          Vintage:

Imported by:

Where tasted:          Date:

Served with:

Clarity, hue, density of color:

Aroma or bouquet:

Taste, texture, balance and harmony:

Other comments:

~ ~ ~ ~ ~ ~ ~ ~ ~ ~ ~ ~ ~ ~ ~ ~ ~ ~ ~ ~

Wine:

Producer:          Vintage:

Imported by:

Where tasted:          Date:

Served with:

Clarity, hue, density of color:

Aroma or bouquet:

Taste, texture, balance and harmony:

Other comments:

Wine: *Castello Della Sala*

Producer: *Umbria*                          Vintage: *2005*

Imported by:                                 *Chardona*

Where tasted:                                Date:

Served with:

Clarity, hue, density of color:

Aroma or bouquet:        *Excellent (*

Taste, texture, balance and harmony:

Other comments:

~ ~ ~ ~ ~ ~ ~ ~ ~ ~ ~ ~ ~ ~ ~ ~ ~ ~ ~ ~ ~ ~ ~ ~

Wine: *Venica IT*

Producer: *Italy*                            Vintage:

Imported by:                    *Pinot Grigio*

Where tasted: *Postino*                      Date:

Served with:

Clarity, hue, density of color:

Aroma or bouquet:

Taste, texture, balance and harmony:

Other comments:

ABBOCCATO: Slightly sweet (used on Italian white wine labels).

AMABILE: Soft, slightly sweet (used on Italian red wine labels).

AMERICAN VITICULTURAL AREA (AVA): A geographically defined area, such as Napa Valley or the North Fork of Long Island, formally recognized by the designated U. S. authority (the Bureau of Alcohol, Tobacco and Firearms) for the effect of its distinctive climatic and geological unity on the style of wines produced there.

APPELLATION D'ORIGINE CONTRÔLÉE: French legal system, established in the 1930s and directed by the *Institut National des Appellations d'Origine,* which defines geographically those place-names within France used to describe wines and which imposes conditions—grape varieties to be used, method of viticulture, permitted yields, parameters of quality—on those who produce them. Similar systems have since been introduced into other countries in Europe and elsewhere, identified by terms such as *denominación de origen* (Spain) and *denominazione d'origine controllata* (Italy).

BLANC DE BLANCS: Originally this expression referred only to Champagne made from white grapes. (Though a white wine, Champagne is normally made from a mixture of black and white grapes.) The words are now sometimes used to describe other still and sparkling wines made from white grapes only.

BOTRYTIS CINEREA (NOBLE ROT, POURRITURE NOBLE, EDELFÄULE, MUFFA NOBILE): the fungus that attacks ripe grapes softened by morning mists. It causes them to shrivel rather than rot, and their concentrated juice is made into luscious and prestigious dessert wines. In California such wines often carry the message "made from botrytized grapes."

CARBONIC MACERATION: A technique in which whole bunches of grapes are held for several days in an atmosphere of carbon dioxide before being crushed. The carbon dioxide is usually generated by bunches at the bottom of the vat fermenting after being crushed by the weight of those above. Lack of oxygen inhibits the yeast that would normally set the whole vat fermenting, and allows a different kind of fermentation to occur within each unbroken grape. This draws flavor and aroma rather than tannin from the grape. As a result, wines made with carbonic maceration are particularly soft and noticeably grapey.

CAVA: This word for cave has been adopted in Spanish law to designate sparkling wines made in Spain by the Champagne method (the second fermentation occurs in the bottle in which the wine is later to be sold).

CHAIS: French word for the above-ground cellars in which wine is stored on a Bordeaux property.

CHAPTALIZATION: The process of adjusting a deficiency in the sugar concentration of ripe grapes when crushed and ready for fermentation. Named for Jean-Antoine Chaptal, the French chemist and statesman who introduced the metric system to France, it was made possible by two developments in the late eighteenth and early nineteenth centuries— the invention of the saccharometer to measure the density of sugar in liquids and the discovery of an industrial technique for extracting sugar cheaply from beets.

CHÂTEAU, DOMAIN, DOMAINE, DOMÄNE, WEINGUT, QUINTA, FATTORIA, TENUTA: Though the meaning of each of these words, in various European languages, has a subtle shading of its own, all, when seen on a wine label, refer to a wine estate.

CLARET: British term for red Bordeaux wine.

CLIMAT: A term applied, most often in Burgundy, to a vineyard site defined by physical characteristics—altitude, exposure, degree of slope— that slightly modify its climate and therefore distinguish it from sites surrounding it.

COLHEITA: Portuguese word used to describe tawny (wood-aged) port sold with a single vintage identity. Most tawny port is blended and cannot be identified as the wine from a particular year.

COOPÉRATIVE, WINZERGENOSSENSCHAFT, CANTINA SOCIALE: European wine cooperatives are owned by their members who continue to tend their individual vineyards but bring their crop to the jointly owned winery facility where it is made into wine by professionally trained personnel using equipment the growers might not have felt justified in purchasing individually.

CORKED: A wine is corked when tainted by the smell and taste of a mold that grows in the pores of affected corks. If spoiled in this way, the wine smells quite distinctly of old, damp cardboard. Small pieces of cork crumb that have fallen into wine can be unsightly, but do not make it corked.

COSECHA: Spanish for vintage date, used to indicate the year the wine was made.

CÔTE, COTEAU: Both words refer to a hill-slope, a preferred location for the production of quality wine.

CRÉMANT: A term that once referred to Champagne made with a bottle pressure slightly lower that the standard five or six atmospheres, and, therefore, less fizzy. It now is used to describe French sparkling wines other than Champagne made by the Champagne-method (involving a second fermentation in the bottle).

CRU: Literally *growth,* it is normally used for á château or estate vineyard of some distinction. It also refers to certain Burgundian and other vineyard sites officially defined and classified as a unit though ownership of the land is divided among several growers. The *crus classés* of Bordeaux are the sixty château-estates classified into five ranks at the Paris Universal Exhibition of 1855.

CUVÉE: Literally *vatfull,* the expression is used mostly when referring to a Champagne blend, but is also often applied to blends of other wines.

DEMI-SEC: Champagne, when first developed as a sparkling wine, was sweet and was served at dessert. *Demi-sec* means half-dry, and the term was used in the nineteenth century to describe Champagnes less sweet than the standard. Today, Champagne is essentially a dry wine served as an aperitif, so that a *demi-sec cuvée,* though remaining what it has always been, is now a Champagne sweeter than the standard. It has taken the place of the old, sweet Champagne (now disappeared) as a wine for pastry and dessert.

DOSAGE: Before Champagne or any other sparkling wine made by the Champagne-method is released for sale, sediment formed during the second fermentation in bottle must be removed and the bottle topped up with similar wine enriched with a little sugar to round out the blend and restore its balance. That sugar adjustment is known as the *dosage*. For a normal *brut* Champagne it is usually between eight and fifteen grammes per liter. (The standard Champagne bottle contains three-quarters of a liter.)

EISWEIN: Wine made from grapes picked when frozen and crushed immediately. They are usually gathered before dawn, and in any case must, by law, be picked when the air temperature in the vineyard is below –8°C. Freezing separates water from natural grape sugars already concentrated by dehydration while the fruit was left hanging on the vine. An *Eiswein* is usually richly concentrated, highly prized, and very expensive.

FERMENTATION: In terms of wine, this refers to the conversion of grape sugar to ethyl alcohol through the action of either yeast present in the atmosphere or selected yeast introduced to the grape juice for that purpose. *See also* MALOLACTIC FERMENTATION

FORTIFIED: Some wines are fortified with alcohol, either after fermentation (as is the case with Sherry), or during fermentation (as is the case with Port and certain other sweet wines in which brandy is used to arrest the process and retain grape sugar in the finished wine). Fortified wines usually have an alcoholic strength of 18 percent or 19 percent, compared with the 11 percent to 13 percent alcoholic strength of most table wines.

GENERIC: A generic wine is one classified by type rather than by geographic origin or variety of grape. In California, generic names were often European place-names borrowed and misused.

KABINETT, SPÄTLESE, AUSLESE, BEERENAUSLESE, TROCKENBEERENAUSLESE: In addition to their geographic definitions by village and vineyard (for example, Niersteiner Brudersberg—where Nierstein is the village and Brudersberg the vineyard site), German wines have definitions of quality based on the degree of grape maturity at harvest expressed in terms of their sugar concentration when picked. Wines made from grapes with particularly low sugars, even though adjusted before fermentation, may be sold only as *Tafelwein* (table wine) and are usually consumed as local carafe wines within Germany. Wines made from grapes with sugar levels above a legally defined acceptable minimum but that still require some slight sugar adjustment are classified as *Qualitätswein* and may carry a reference to geographic origin but nothing more. Those requiring no sugar adjustment at all are known as *Qualitätswein mit Prädikat,* a term which can be translated loosely as "quality wine with description." They are usually referred to simply as *Prädikat* wines, and the descriptions they carry, each defined by the concentration of sugar in the grapes from which they are made, rise from *Kabinett* through *Spätlese, Auslese,* and *Beerenauslese* to *Trockenbeerenauslese. Kabinett* wines are usually fermented dry, but can sometimes have a trace of residual sugar for balance. *Spätlese* wines are usually mild, with a slightly sweet finish, but are sometimes quite dry (usually indicated by the word *Trocken).* From *Auslese* to *Trockenbeerenauslese* one expects to find increasing levels of residual sugar in the wine.

MALOLACTIC FERMENTATION: A secondary fermentation in young wine, bacterially provoked, that converts harsh malic acid into mild lactic acid, thereby softening the wine. It can also help unify disparate qualities in a wine, rather as a final wash does when applied to a finished watercolor.

MILLÉSIME: A French term for a wine's vintage, its year of production.

MIS EN BOUTEILLE: French for bottled. The German equivalent is *Abfüllung.*

MOELLEUX: A French term meaing mellow, applied to white wines that are off-dry.

MOUSSEUX: Sparkling wine, usually one made by a method other than the classic *méthde champenoise,* with a second fermentation in the bottle.

MUST: The crushed mass of juice, seeds and skin, or the separated juice of white grapes, to be fermented into wine.

NÉGOCIANT: A merchant who buys wines for blending and sale under his own label, or grapes for fermenting into wine in his own cellars to be sold under his own name.

OXIDIZE: The attachment of oxygen to components of wine. In controlled measure, it can add to a wine's depth of flavor, but when caused by excessive exposure to air it is detrimental to quality.

PHYLLOXERA: A louse that feeds on vine roots. European vines—the familiar *vinifera* varieties such as Chardonnay and Cabernet Sauvignon—are vulnerable to its depredations and must therefore be grown as grafts on rootstocks of American varieties which are either resistant to or tolerant of *phylloxera*—which is why such vines still exist in the first place. *Phylloxera* is native to North America and was taken to Europe inadvertently in the 1860s.

PRIMEUR: In France, the wines of a new vintage are allowed to enter the market on or after December 15; exceptions are made for certain wines— among them Beaujolais Nouveau—which may be sold a month earlier and are therefore referred to as *primeur.*

PROPRIÉTAIRE: Owner, the proprietor of a vineyard.

RÉCOLTE: The harvest; sometimes used in the sense of "vintage" or "year."

RESERVE, RESERVA, RISERVA: In many countries this word means as much or as little as the producer chooses. In California it sometimes means a special, superior bottling, but it is also used by some wineries to designate their wine of carafe quality. In Italy and Spain, *Riserva* and *Reserva* are used to indicate red wines that, in compliance with the legal requirements of a controlled appellation, have been aged longer.

SEC, SECCO, SECO: Dry.

SEKT: German for sparkling wine.

SULFITES: As used on wine labels this is a catchall term for any form of sulfur or sulfur compounds in wine. Sulfur exists naturally in our bodies and in much of what we eat (in eggs and in onions, for example). Even in the ancient world, it was used to purify barrels and other wine containers, and has for centuries been an effective treatment for maladies of the vine. At low levels it is also sometimes used as an antioxidant in wine. It is rare for a wine to have more than twenty parts per million free sulfur.

SÜSSRESERVE: Unfermented grape juice, usually concentrated, is used in Germany to adjust the final balance of sugar and acid in some wines prior to bottling. As drier German wines gain favor, so the use of *Süssreserve* is diminishing, particularly among quality growers.

TANNIN: Though used in the singular, tannin, like acid, exists in many forms. Tannin in wine is derived mostly from the grape skins, but also from seeds and stems. When present in excess, or derived from unripe skins or stalks, tannins give an astringent and even bitter taste to wine. When fully mature, they usually add to the wine's structure, body, and texture. The level of tannin varies with the grape variety as well as with wine-making technique. Cabernet Sauvignon grapes, for example, contribute far more tannin than do Pinot Noir grapes.

TARTRATES: Tartrates sometimes appear as a sparkling dust clinging to the underside of the cork or as tiny rocklike fragments in the wine. Either way, they are harmless. Tartaric acid, specific to grapes and wine, combines with potassium and sodium, also naturally present, to form potassium and sodium tartrates. Most of it is deposited in the tanks, vats, and barrels where wine is fermented and aged (the wine industry is the only source of tartrates for industrial use), but a continuing slow deposit is likely during the years in bottle. Tartrates form much of the bottle sediment in old wines.

TERROIR: A French term intended to include a vineyard's entire ecological environment. Sometimes assumed to mean *soil* (because of confusion with the French word *terre,* land) *terroir,* as applied to a vineyard, also means the life in the soil; its situation (altitude, exposure, surroundings) and climate; as well as the history of the soil—the way it has been physically affected by centuries of cultivation and local growing practices. As far as a vineyard is concerned, man himself is part of the environment.

ULLAGE: The unfilled space at the top of a bottle of wine, or the space that remains unfilled in a wine barrel.

VARIETAL: A varietal is a wine made from and named for a specific variety of grape—Chardonnay, for example, Merlot, or Cabernet Franc. In California a varietal wine must contain a minimum of 75 per cent of the named grape.

VECCHIO: Old—but when applied to Italian wine it usually means any wine that is not new, that is, any wine older than one year.

VENDANGE TARDIVE: Like California's Late Harvest, this expression, used in Alsace, means that the grapes were allowed to hang longer so that, by overripening, or by dehydration, or by *botrytis,* they would be richer in sugar. Usually, some of that sugar remains in the wine when fermentation is over, ensuring a luscious—but unfortified—dessert wine.

VIGNERON: A small winegrower

VIGNOBLE: Used as a collective noun for vineyards, especially those of an entire region. One refers, for example, to the *vignoble* of Saint-Emilion, meaning the vineyards of Saint-Emilion, and even *le vignoble français,* the vineyards of France.

VIÑA, VINHA: In Spanish and Portuguese respectively, words used to designate a single vineyard.

VINTAGE: The word means wine harvest, but is more often used to specify a particular year; so that a vintage 1989 Château Haut-Brion means a wine grown and made in 1989.

NOTES:

*Rodney Stone + St. Francis in Sonoma County*

*Grocery Outlet*

*Craftwork - 2012 —*
*2014 Chenan Blanc . OK*
*Goss Creek Chardonay*
*Speckicle 2013 ← Not Good*